D1522298

MARTIN LUTHER KING JR.

Civil Rights Leader

MARTIN LUTHER
KING JR.

Civil Rights Leader

BY KRISTINE CARLSON ASSELIN

CONTENT CONSULTANT
PAUL ORTIZ
SAMUEL PROCTOR ORAL HISTORY PROGRAM
ASSOCIATE PROFESSOR OF HISTORY
UNIVERSITY OF FLORIDA

CREDITS

Published by ABDO Publishing Company, PO Box 398166, Minneapolis, MN 55439. Copyright © 2014 by Abdo Consulting Group, Inc. International copyrights reserved in all countries. No part of this book may be reproduced in any form without written permission from the publisher. The Essential Library™ is a trademark and logo of ABDO Publishing Company.

Printed in the United States of America,
North Mankato, Minnesota
052013
092013

 THIS BOOK CONTAINS AT LEAST 10% RECYCLED MATERIALS.

Editor: Rebecca Rowell
Series Designer: Becky Daum

Photo credits: Consolidated News Pictures/Getty Images, cover, 2; Bettmann/Corbis/ AP Images, 6, 41, 47, 51, 52, 69, 70, 73; AP Images, 13, 14, 21, 22, 36, 42, 59, 60, 63, 66, 79, 80, 83, 86, 89; Carol M. Highsmith, 29, 30; Horace Cort/AP Images, 95

Library of Congress Control Number: 2013932920

Cataloging-in-Publication Data

Asselin, Kristine Carlson.
 Martin Luther King Jr. : civil rights leader / Kristine Carlson Asselin.
  p. cm. -- (Essential lives)
ISBN 978-1-61783-891-0
Includes bibliographical references and index.
1. King, Martin Luther, Jr., 1929-1968--Juvenile literature. 2. African Americans-- Biography--Juvenile literature. 3. Civil rights workers--United States--Biography-- Juvenile literature. 4. Baptists--United States--Clergy--Biography--Juvenile literature. I. Title.
323/.092--dc23
[B]   2013932920

CONTENTS

CHAPTER
ONE

THE BUS BOYCOTT

M artin Luther King Jr. and his wife, Coretta, watched from their window as a city bus made its way down the street in the early morning darkness. At 5:30 a.m., the bus was usually crowded with commuters. But on December 5, 1955, as it approached the stop just outside the couple's house, the bus was empty. They were stunned—the people were supporting the boycott.

After the third empty bus drove by, King took his car to see if buses were empty in other parts of the city. Driving through Montgomery, Alabama, he noticed the sidewalks packed with walkers. College students hitched rides. People going to work hiked up to 12 miles (19 km) round-trip. Taxis drove people to their destinations for reduced rates. He said of the event later, "As I watched them, I knew that there is nothing more majestic than the determined courage of individuals willing to suffer and sacrifice for their freedom and dignity."[1]

Rosa Parks rides at the front of a Montgomery city bus legally in December 1956, a year after doing so got her arrested.

Sitting at the Back of the Bus

In 1955, 50,000 of Montgomery's 130,000 residents were African Americans. And they did not have the same rights as the city's white citizens.

At age 26, King was no stranger to discrimination. The intelligent young man who had graduated from college at age 19 and was the respected pastor of the most influential church in the city's African-American community had faced harassment and name-calling because of his race.

King also knew the sting of not having the choice to sit where he wanted on the bus. He had experienced being forced from a seat because a white person wanted it.

Perhaps King remembered his own experiences when he heard about Rosa Parks. The Montgomery seamstress and community organizer refused to give up her seat on the bus when asked on December 1, 1955. She was arrested and fined ten dollars, plus an additional four dollars for court costs. Her action was the catalyst for the city's African-American community. Montgomery's black citizens were tired of the treatment they received in their own town. They were tired of being told where to stand when a white person got on the bus. They were tired of using separate public bathrooms. They were tired of being called names. They had had enough and wanted something different. They wanted better. They were ready to take a stand, and King agreed to lead their fight for equality.

Continuing the Boycott

On December 5, some African-American leaders, mostly from local churches, met with members of the Women's Political Council (WPC) to discuss how

ROSA PARKS

Rosa Parks did not set out to be a key character in a pivotal moment in US history, but she had challenged Jim Crow laws before. Parks had led a group of black students to demand the right to check out books from whites-only libraries in 1949.

On December 1, 1955, the 42-year-old seamstress climbed onto the bus after work and sat in the first seat in the section reserved for black patrons. At the next stop, the bus driver told Parks and several other black riders to give up their seats to white customers. She refused and was arrested. Later, Parks described her experience on the bus:

When that white driver . . . ordered us up and out of our seats, I felt a determination cover my body like a quilt on a winter night. I felt all the meanness of every white driver I'd seen who'd been ugly to me and other black people through the years I'd known on the buses in Montgomery. I felt a light suddenly shine through the darkness.[2]

During the boycott, Parks helped organize rides for people. She also made public appearances in churches and other public places to raise awareness of the event.

to keep the bus boycott moving forward. One local activist, E. B. Nixon, once led the local chapter of the National Association for the Advancement of Colored People (NAACP). Nixon had bailed Parks out of jail. He and the WPC had been planning a citywide bus boycott in Montgomery since 1953, and Parks's arrest was the perfect catalyst to launch it.

After some deliberation, the organizing group formed the Montgomery Improvement Association (MIA) to officially coordinate boycott efforts. The group also elected King president of the new organization.

The one-day boycott had worked so well, MIA leaders wondered if they could keep it going. If the boycott continued, it would cost the bus company money. After all, most of the bus company's revenue—more than 70 percent—came from its African-American customers. Losing money might get the owners to agree to change the rule about African Americans riding at the back of the bus. The MIA's first vote was to continue the bus boycott until the bus company agreed to meet the group's demands for fair treatment for all citizens. The MIA wanted guaranteed courteous treatment by bus drivers and for passengers to be seated on a first-come, first-served basis: black patrons from the back forward, white patrons from front to back. The organization also demanded the company hire blacks to drive the routes frequented primarily by black patrons.

When it became clear the company would not cooperate with the MIA, leaders went to work. They collaborated with the WPC. Nixon, an MIA member, helped by giving the MIA contact information for a variety of civil rights and labor groups. They, in turn, gave the cause money and political support. Jo Ann Robinson and a team of teachers from Alabama State College and the public school system headed the WPC. Nixon and the WPC arranged transportation and communication efforts during the boycott. More than 200 volunteers provided in excess of 20,000 rides a day to help people get around the city. Many of the volunteers and boycotters were poor and did not own cars. They were working people, including maids, porters, custodians, and laborers. By participating in the

SEGREGATION

After the American Civil War (1861–1865), Congress passed the Civil Rights Act of 1875 to outlaw discrimination in hotels, trains, and other public places. However, in 1883, the US Supreme Court ruled the Civil Rights Act of 1875 unconstitutional. Overturning the law meant state governments could legally impose segregation laws to keep blacks and whites separate. There would not be another civil rights act until 1957.

boycott, they risked violence and retaliation.

Fighting without Violence

Of utmost importance to King was that the protest be nonviolent. He believed even violence in self-defense was wrong. He knew an open revolt against a powerful majority would be suicidal. He felt the only solution to effect the change they wanted was passive, nonviolent resistance.

Even when his own home was bombed in January 1956, King urged his followers to find forgiveness for the perpetrators. He said, "We are not advocating violence. . . . I want you to love our enemies. Be good to them. Love them and let them know you love them."[3] The angry crowd dispersed.

In late 1956, the US Supreme Court ruled Alabama's laws requiring segregation on buses unconstitutional. After 381 days and near complete participation by the city's African-American community, the boycott was

"The end of violence or the aftermath of violence is bitterness. The aftermath of nonviolence is reconciliation and the creation of a beloved community. A boycott is never an end within itself. It is merely a means to awaken a sense of shame within the oppressor but the end is reconciliation, the end is redemption."[4]
—Martin Luther King Jr., "The Power of Nonviolence," June 4, 1957, University of California, Berkeley

Martin Luther King Jr., *back left*, and colleague Ralph Abernathy, *front left*, ride a desegregated bus in Montgomery in December 1956.

over. King urged the people of Montgomery to go back to the buses "with humility and meekness," not bragging about beating the system.[5] He wanted them to take the moral high ground. He also stressed integration based on mutual respect.

On December 21, 1956, the buses of Montgomery were integrated. The city was forever changed, and the activists' victory would inspire countless others throughout the world in their own fights for justice. King emerged as a thoughtful and inspirational leader. He would soon gain national and international fame, urging racial, social, and economic equality for all. He was ready to rise to history.

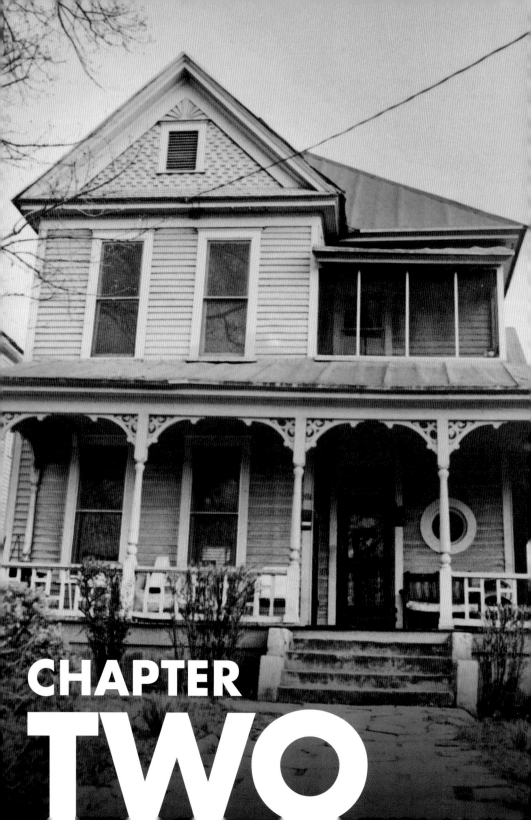

CHAPTER
TWO

YOUNG MARTIN

Martin Luther King Jr. was born on January 15, 1929, in Atlanta, Georgia. His birth name was Michael but he was soon called Martin. He was the second child of Alberta King and Martin Luther King Sr. The couple had three children. Christine was born in 1927, and Alfred Daniel was born in 1930.

Martin's birth coincided with the beginning of the Great Depression, but his family never suffered from hunger or poverty. Alberta served as a teacher until Christine was born. In 1931, Martin's father inherited the leadership of the Ebenezer Baptist Church from his own father-in-law, having served as the assistant pastor. By saving money and living modestly, the family survived the Depression in relative comfort.

The King family lived in a modest middle-class neighborhood called Sweet Auburn. It was an active area for Atlanta's African-American community. Sweet Auburn had many small businesses, a university campus,

Martin grew up in a comfortable home in a friendly Atlanta neighborhood.

and several churches and cafés. It was easy to feel insulated from the hostilities of racism.

Martin grew up in the house where his mother was raised. The backyard was often busy with neighborhood games of football and baseball. Martin was a good athlete, but he loved words more than sports, even as a child. He enjoyed listening to his father preach to the congregation. Watching the people respond to the emotional words, weeping or shouting in response to the sermon, fascinated Martin.

Alberta and Martin Sr. tried to shield their children as much as possible from discrimination. But in many parts of the United States in the early and middle 1900s, especially in the South, having dark skin meant being treated like a second-class citizen.

Facing Discrimination for the First Time

When he was six years old, Martin faced the harsh reality of discrimination for the first time. His best friend was the son of the neighborhood grocery store owner. Until they were old enough to start school, the boys played together almost every day. That changed when the two boys started going to school. Martin and his friend went to different schools. Martin's friend was white. Because of segregation, the two could not legally attend the same school. They could have played with each other outside of school, except the father of Martin's friend would no longer allow it because Martin was black.

Alberta explained to her young son why segregation and discrimination existed in the world. She made sure Martin knew he was "as good as anybody" even though he lived in a society that treated him as though he were not.[1] The little boy was sad and shocked to hear his parents' stories about being insulted and harassed. He was determined to hate white people for taking away his friend. His parents insisted that because of their Christian faith, he must love everyone. Martin had trouble understanding this because he was so young.

JIM CROW LAWS

After the American Civil War, until the mid-1960s, many states and cities used Jim Crow laws to enforce segregation. Named after an African-American character in minstrel shows, these laws mandated that businesses and other public places keep black customers and white customers separate. In 1896, the US Supreme Court ruled segregation was legal as long as the accommodations were of equal quality. Jim Crow laws varied by state and prohibited blacks and whites from doing a variety of activities together, including playing cards and checkers, sitting in the same area of a train, and attending school.

Because Martin Sr. was the leader of an important church and involved in local civil rights organizations, he occasionally received threatening telephone calls and letters. He faced these threats and other mistreatment with simmering rage. Once, he said to young Martin, "I don't care how long I have to live with this system, I am never going to accept it. I'll oppose it until the day I die."[2] Martin Sr. fought to desegregate the elevators in the Atlanta courthouse and to get equal pay for African-American teachers. Martin learned well from his parents and took their teachings to heart.

AN UNFORGETTABLE EVENT

When he was 14 years old, Martin participated in a speaking competition in Dublin, Georgia. He traveled to the event by bus with a teacher, Mrs. Brady. His subject for the competition was "The Negro and the Constitution." He won.

On the ride home, the bus driver insisted Martin and Mrs. Brady give their seats to two white passengers who had boarded. When Martin and his teacher did not move fast enough to give over their seats, the bus driver got upset and began to swear at them. The 14-year-old decided he would stay put and not give up his seat, but Mrs. Brady intervened. She told Martin to get up and that the two had to follow the law. Martin and his teacher rode standing for the 90-mile (145 km) trip back to Atlanta.

Martin later wrote about the event. The incident left an indelible mark on him: "That night will never leave my memory. It was the angriest I have ever been in my life."[3]

An Exceptional Student

Martin excelled as a student. He skipped two grades in high school to start college when he was 15. He attended Morehouse College in Atlanta, his father's alma mater. The all-men's school was famous for graduating leaders in the African-American community. Morehouse expected its graduates to succeed—and from the first day, Martin loved the social and political climate of the campus. Students were encouraged to talk with peers and teachers alike and to learn as much as they could about the world.

Martin was not sure what profession to choose. Part of him wanted to be a minister, like his father and grandfather. But he did not care for the overly emotional nature of the church—hand clapping and "amen-ing."[4] At the time, such public displays embarrassed him because he thought it fed into a cartoonish image of African Americans as loud and lacking dignity. Martin wanted to address the social conditions of the African-American community and thought he could do that more successfully as a lawyer. He decided to major in sociology and pursue law.

While he was a college student, Martin traveled outside of Georgia for the first time. In the summer of 1944, he worked with other youth on a tobacco farm near Hartford, Connecticut. He was pleased to notice the absence of Jim Crow signs that signaled segregation. He was treated differently, too.

Martin was enraged when, upon returning to Atlanta on the train, he was forced to sit behind a curtain because he was black. This experience made him even more convinced he wanted to be a lawyer. Martin would need to excel at public speaking. Even though he had already won awards for public speaking, he started to practice giving speeches in front of a mirror.

In his junior year, Martin decided not to become a lawyer. Two high-profile leaders of Morehouse were ministers: president Benjamin Mays and director of religion George D. Kelsey. Both men preached in a style Martin felt was ideal for a minister—"socially relevant and intellectually stimulating."[5] He decided to follow in his mentors' footsteps.

Martin analyzed his feelings about the highly emotional nature of the church and vowed to be a rational minister. Mays's sermons on social justice and racial equality and his ardent opposition to war inspired

Martin, *second from left*, as a student at Morehouse College, where speakers shaped the leader he would become

young Martin's own personal philosophy. Martin believed the ministry would be the best platform for him to share his own ideas for social change. Martin made up his mind. He would pursue civil justice from the pulpit.

WHY WE CAN'T WAIT

WHY WE CAN'T WAIT

MARTIN LUTHER KING, JR

CHAPTER
THREE

FINDING A CAREER, INSPIRATION, AND LOVE

King's decision to be a minister delighted his father. King delivered his first sermon at Ebenezer Baptist Church, where his father served as minister. The congregants loved him. King was ordained the assistant pastor of the church on February 25, 1948. He was only 18 years old and still in college.

Discovering His Inspiration

Back at Morehouse, King discovered the writings of Henry David Thoreau. Thoreau was an American writer in the 1800s who believed in civil disobedience as a strategy for protesting the wrongs in the world. King began to think about how to use peaceful noncooperation to protest segregation. Thoreau's ideas remained with King when he graduated from Morehouse

In addition to his speeches and actions, King inspired others with his written words.

and enrolled at Crozer Theological Seminary in Chester, Pennsylvania, in 1948.

As always, King was a good student—he held an A average for all three years he studied at Crozer. He enjoyed his classes and made friends with his white classmates. And he was the first African-American student to serve as senior class president.

But things were not always easy for King. Even in the Northeast, where blacks and whites were not

KING'S BEHAVIOR AT CROZER

While attending Crozer Theological Seminary, King was in a small minority. Of the more than 100 students in his class, there were only six African Americans. Feeling as though he represented all African Americans, the young man tried hard to exceed any expectations his classmates may have had because of any stereotypes they might have held against blacks. He did not want to behave in the ways whites deemed typical of black men, such as being consistently loud and late or seeming to laugh constantly.

With this stereotype in mind, King went to the extreme and behaved in an opposite manner to avoid association with it. King wrote about this experience:

If I were a minute late to class, I was almost morbidly conscious of it and sure that everyone else noticed it. Rather than being thought of as always laughing, I'm afraid I was grimly serious for a time. I had a tendency to overdress, to keep my room spotless, my shoes perfectly shined, and my clothes immaculately pressed.[1]

segregated, discrimination was common. Just as many of his African-American peers did, King experienced harassment. Once, he and some friends were declined service at a restaurant in New Jersey. When they refused to leave, the restaurant owner waved a gun to threaten them. King responded by using the strategy the NAACP recommended. The friends called the police, had the owner arrested, and filed a lawsuit. In the end, the witnesses refused to testify and the police closed the case.

The Power of Love

While attending Crozer, King thought about using force to end segregation. He believed the tactic of love would work only in individual relationships, not for a large battle such as ending discrimination.

Such thoughts of violence did not last long. While still at Crozer, King attended a sermon by Mordecai Johnson, president of Howard University, a traditionally black school in Washington, DC. Johnson was a minister and powerful orator on the issues of racism, discrimination, and segregation. He spoke at length about a pilgrimage to India and the teachings of Mohandas Gandhi. Johnson's words inspired King, who left the speech and immediately bought an armful of books about Gandhi's life and message. King embraced Gandhi's philosophy about the power of love and nonviolence as the only viable method for social reform.

King graduated from Crozer in 1951. He decided he wanted to teach religion at the college level someday. He knew he needed additional education to reach this goal and enrolled at Boston University in Massachusetts for his doctoral degree.

At Boston University, King connected with a fellow Morehouse graduate who helped shape his philosophy. Howard Thurman was the dean of Boston University's Marsh Chapel. Thurman underscored the idea of nonviolence as a strategy against injustice and evil. He also embraced Gandhi's teachings. Thurman urged King to maintain a spiritual life while fighting for social change.

Meeting Coretta Scott

Attending Boston University also put King in the same city as Coretta Scott, which would prove to be one of the best coincidences of his life. Coretta was a young music student at New England Conservatory. She shared King's passion for combating social injustices.

The two students met through a mutual friend in late January 1952. At first, Coretta was not interested because she heard King was a minister. Although she considered herself very religious, she had strayed from her childhood church and did not attend church in Boston.

Coretta's lack of a strong religious life did not bother King. He was convinced she was the right one for him an hour after they met.

Coretta's negative first impression of the short, stocky young minister did not last long. His charismatic personality and humor made her want to see him again—even though his talk of marriage on their first date flustered her.

Soon after their first date, King told his mother he was going to marry Coretta. And he did. On June 18, 1953, King's father married the couple at the bride's family home in Marion, Alabama. After the wedding, the newlyweds returned to Boston to finish their education.

Back to Alabama

By 1954, King had invitations to serve several churches. He chose Dexter Avenue Baptist Church in Montgomery, Alabama. Coretta knew life would not be easy in that part of the country. Coretta wanted to stay in the North—discrimination still existed, but it was not all encompassing as in the South. But King believed he was meant to be the pastor of a southern church. A sense of purpose seemed to be pulling them toward their future. She said later, "We felt a sense of destiny, of being propelled in a certain

Dexter Avenue Baptist Church

positive direction."[2] Choosing to make their home in
Montgomery was the start of a tumultuous life together
that would bring the Kings international recognition.

CHAPTER
FOUR

INTO THE NATIONAL SPOTLIGHT

King began his work as pastor of Dexter Avenue Baptist Church in May 1954, working part-time as he finished his doctoral thesis. He took on full-time responsibilities on September 1. King's commitment to following in the footsteps of his mentors and making social justice the central theme of his ministry was evident in his first sermon to his congregation that spring:

> It is a significant fact that I come to the pastorate of Dexter at a most crucial hour of our world's history; at a time when the flame of war might arise at any time to redden the skies of our dark and dreary world; at a time when men know all too well that without the proper guidance the whole of civilization can be plunged across the abyss of destruction.[1]

King inspired many with the sermons he gave from the pulpit of the Dexter Avenue Baptist Church.

King spent hours practicing his sermons and often spoke about social action to his congregation. He encouraged congregants to join committee groups and register to vote.

The Beginning of Social Change

At the time, the atmosphere in the country surrounding segregation and discrimination was tense. Social change moved very slowly. Earlier that year, in May, the US Supreme Court had ordered schools to desegregate in the landmark case *Brown v. Board of Education*. This ruling was a monumental win for equal rights. The NAACP had been fighting for school equality for decades. And NAACP Legal Fund lawyers such as Charles Hamilton Houston and Thurgood Marshall, who would become a Supreme Court justice, made *Brown* possible. As a result of the ruling, black children could legally attend the schools in their own neighborhoods that had been designated for whites only. However, just because segregation was outlawed did not mean getting to the schools would be easy for African-American children.

Some people believed whites and blacks should be separate, including a variety of lawmakers and state governments. To continue segregation, some southern states argued they had the right to invoke states rights. They claimed the right to make local policies to allow school districts to preserve racial segregation into the 1970s.

Other white citizens who opposed the Supreme Court's decision joined hate groups whose sole purpose was to scare people and delay integration and equality. Part of the mission of these groups, including the Ku Klux Klan (KKK), was to frighten African-American community members and anyone who supported social justice and equality. In some cases, members of these groups hurt or killed African Americans as well as anyone trying to protest inequality.

Leaders in the African-American community—mostly ministers and community organizers—struggled with how to proceed. There were various opinions about how to stand up to these racist groups. As a respected minister of a large church, King had a big

BECOMING DR. KING

While King was busy being a husband, father, pastor, and civil rights leader, he also continued to be a student. He was working on his doctoral degree in systematic theology. He received his PhD from Boston University on June 5, 1955, making him Dr. King.

voice in Montgomery. Though he accepted his role, he sometimes worried about finding a balance between keeping people "courageous and prepared for positive action and yet devoid of hate and resentment."[2]

When the issue of the bus boycott came up in December 1955, King was in the right place to accept the presidency of the MIA. He said,

> I became convinced that what we were preparing to do in Montgomery was related to what Thoreau had expressed. We were simply saying to the white community, "we can no longer lend our cooperation to an evil system." From this moment on, I conceived of our movement as an act of massive noncooperation.[3]

Three weeks before the beginning of the Montgomery bus boycott, the Kings became parents when Yolanda Denise was born on November 17. Life was very stressful, but the baby gave King a much-needed distraction from the pressures he faced on a daily basis.

The success of the bus boycott proved to King and his followers that peaceful noncooperation could work. But the method was not without its opponents. Some people approached King to suggest they should hurt a few white people in retaliation for the violence against blacks. Others felt they could remain nonviolent only if opponents did not attack first—but they would fight back if attacked. King remained firm in his belief in nonviolence without exception, and most of his followers were willing to try it, too.

The Southern Christian Leadership Conference

Violence from hate groups continued to accelerate as more and more institutions became integrated. In the late 1950s and early 1960s, it was common to hear white segregationists had bombed churches, schools, and private homes of community leaders.

In January 1957, the morning after touring the remains of two bombed churches in Montgomery, King flew to Atlanta. He and close colleagues C. K. Steele and Fred Shuttlesworth had invited 100 African-American leaders from across the South to discuss options for implementing integration. Steele

"Along the way of life, someone must have sense enough and morality enough to cut off the chain of hate and evil. The greatest way to do that is through love. I believe firmly that love is a transforming power that can lift a whole community to new horizons of fair play, good will, and justice."[4]
—Martin Luther King Jr., "Walk for Freedom," Fellowship, May 1956

King, *center*, and Ralph Abernathy, *left*, were colleagues and friends, supporting each other and other activists during their fight for civil rights.

was from Tallahassee, Florida, and Shuttlesworth was from Birmingham, Alabama. The group formed the Southern Christian Leadership Conference (SCLC). Members made two important decisions. They agreed to contact the president of the United States, Dwight

D. Eisenhower, and urge him to speak out against ongoing resistance to integration. And they elected King president of their organization.

Despite the violence acted upon African Americans throughout the South, the SCLC maintained a commitment to work against segregation through nonviolent methods. But King felt discouraged. In January 1957, the church and home of his friend Ralph Abernathy were bombed. No one was injured, but King felt personal responsibility for much of the violence that continued to occur.

More bombings, including his own home for a second time, inspired him to say,

> We must not return violence under any condition. I know this is difficult advice to follow, especially since we have been the victims of no less than ten bombings. . . . We must somehow believe that unearned suffering is redemptive.[5]

Despite the danger to their family and the harassment they received, the Kings were glad they had come to Montgomery. They knew the movement was escalating and becoming national. Coretta said to King one night, "How happy I am to be living in Montgomery, with you, at this moment in history."[6]

International Recognition

In February 1957, *Time* magazine ran a cover article about King and how his leadership had transformed Montgomery. Soon, invitations to speak and to meet with world leaders poured in from around the globe. Prime Minister Kwame Nkrumah of Ghana invited King to the ceremony celebrating that country's independence from British rule. The Kings attended. The couple also visited Nigeria, Italy, Switzerland, France, and England to speak.

After returning from the international tour, King received the first of many prestigious awards. The NAACP awarded him the Spingarn Medal for "the person making the greatest contribution in the field of race relations."[7]

While King was being acknowledged for his civil rights work, portions of the United States continued to oppose laws banning segregation. In some places, police forces and local government officials were part of the groups opposing integration. King felt President Eisenhower and his administration were not moving fast enough on legislation to guarantee African Americans the opportunity to vote. He wanted to put pressure on the US government and decided to visit Washington, DC.

Continuing to Fight for Civil Rights

By May 17, 1957, many southern states had not yet embraced equality and integration. Rather, some states continued to find ways to oppress and keep blacks and whites separate. To mark the third anniversary of the ruling in *Brown v. Board of Education*, more than 30,000 people traveled to the nation's capital as part of the Prayer Pilgrimage for Freedom. Black and white

THE LITTLE ROCK NINE

The Supreme Court's 1954 ruling in *Brown v. Board of Education* made it legal for black children to attend schools once designated as for whites only. Doing so was not always easy or safe. In some cases, mobs of white people or even police authorized by town or city leadership forcibly blocked children from entering formerly whites-only schools.

In 1957, a group of nine African-American students volunteered to test desegregation by enrolling in Little Rock Central High School in Little Rock, Arkansas. The group, who would become known as the Little Rock Nine, tried to get to school on the first day of classes, but they were stopped. The Arkansas National Guard, called out by Governor Orval Faubus, blocked them from entering the school. Angry townspeople taunted some of the African-American students as they tried to get back to their school bus.

President Eisenhower ordered members of the US Army to escort the children into the school on September 25, 1957. Army troops remained on campus the entire school year to ensure the African-American teenagers' safety. All but one of the students completed the school year.

proponents of civil rights gathered to support the cause and protest ongoing oppression. It was the largest civil rights demonstration yet organized and the first time King addressed a national audience.

That year, US Congress passed the Civil Rights Act of 1957. It was the first civil rights legislation since Reconstruction after the Civil War. Unfortunately, the new law was not effective in providing voting rights to African Americans. The law was not worded as strongly as those that would follow, but it was a small victory that demonstrated increasingly growing support from the federal government.

A Blessing and a Near Tragedy

In the midst of these small victories on the national level, the Kings welcomed their second child to the world on October 23, 1957: Martin Luther King III. Less than a year later, King traveled to New York City to promote his first book, *Stride Toward Freedom*. While signing autographs on September 20, 1958, an African-American woman stabbed King in the chest with a letter opener. She babbled nonsensically as members of the crowd subdued her. King remained calm, the

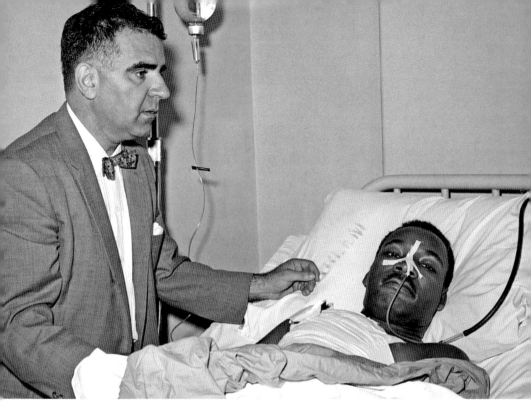

Dr. Emil A. Naclerio tended to King at a hospital in Harlem following the activist's stabbing.

sharp object sticking out of his chest until surgeons could operate.

Later, doctors told Coretta, "The point of the knife was just touching his aorta. If he had moved suddenly, if he had sneezed, he would have died instantly."[8]

King's attacker, Izola Curry, was committed to the Mattewan State Hospital for the Criminally Insane. The attack slowed him down, but only briefly. It made King more committed than ever to maintaining his nonviolent philosophy. He would continue fighting for equality, and he would do it on a larger scale.

CHAPTER
FIVE

GOING TO THE NEXT LEVEL

For years, King had embraced the techniques of love and nonviolent social change taught by Gandhi. In early 1959, after recovering from the attack in New York City, King decided the time was right for a trip to India. He, Coretta, and a small entourage spent more than a month touring and speaking all over India. He had the opportunity to share his views with thousands of Indians. All kinds of people came to hear him, including students and politicians, sometimes in large groups. Coretta participated as well, singing spirituals where King lectured.

King was moved by the poverty and suffering he saw in India. At the same time, he was surprised by the relatively low crime rate. Though many people lived in close quarters and were half starved, they did not act out their frustrations on each other. King thought this behavior was the legacy of Gandhi's teachings.

King and his wife, Coretta, during their visit to India, home of King's inspiration, Gandhi

"This is not the life I expected to lead. But gradually you take some responsibility, then a little more, until finally you are not in control anymore. You have to give yourself entirely."[1]
—Martin Luther King Jr., in a conversation with Coretta, September 3, 1958

King returned home from India to a country still unstable. Violent acts across the South marked the year 1959. White hate groups, attempting to delay integration and defy the federal government, continued their aggression. They bombed property, kidnapped African Americans, and sometimes lynched them. African-American youth groups staged marches and sit-ins to protest how slowly desegregation of the South was happening. Militant African-American organizations were cropping up, and these new groups were not opposed to using violence in retaliation.

Returning to Atlanta

King made a difficult decision that fall. He resigned from the Dexter Avenue Baptist Church. He hated to leave Montgomery—this community had included his most vocal supporters and had performed bravely throughout the bus boycott. However, he felt he needed to commit himself to helping the entire South and that he could do so more effectively from Atlanta.

By taking the role of copastor with his father at
the Ebenezer Baptist Church in Atlanta, King could
give more time to the SCLC and commit more
fully to the fight for civil rights. His congregation in
Montgomery understood. Even so, a number of church
members refused to accept his resignation. King broke
down in tears as the choir sang after his last sermon
in Montgomery.

After resigning from Dexter Avenue Baptist Church,
King threw himself into the civil rights movement. By
moving to Atlanta, he planned to take the fight against
discrimination and segregation to the next level.

In December 1959, King announced, "The time
has come for a broad, bold advance of the southern
campaign for equality."[2] He felt the time was right
to train new leaders and get more people involved in
the nonviolent movement. He knew asking people to
continue protesting meant the leadership needed to be
willing to suffer as well. He was prepared to go to jail
if necessary.

A New Form of Protest

In February 1960, King moved his family to Atlanta
and he began his work as assistant pastor of Ebenezer

Baptist Church. That same month, as if in response to King's call to action, a new form of protest began cropping up, when four black male students from North Carolina Agricultural and Technical College sat down at a Woolworth's lunch counter designated for whites in Greensboro, North Carolina. When employees denied the students service and asked them to leave, the young men refused. They returned to the lunch counter every day, refusing to leave each time. The sit-in lasted six months and ended when the lunch counter was desegregated on July 25. All over the South, others started using the same strategy in their protests against racism.

The sit-in movement was not King's idea, but it was a direct result of his philosophy of nonviolent protest as a powerful tool for social change. Many students at sit-ins carried signs that said, "Remember the teachings of Gandhi and Martin Luther King."[3] King took up the cause by supporting and publicizing the movement.

In October 1960, a group of students in Atlanta asked King to join them at a sit-in at Rich's department store. He enthusiastically agreed. Police arrested King and 280 other protesters. The students were released, but King was charged with violating probation

Coretta and children Yolanda and Martin greet King after his release from prison.

stipulations he received a month before for a traffic violation. He was sentenced to six months of hard labor at Georgia State Prison. He would not serve the full sentence.

Politics

In late 1960, John F. Kennedy and Richard M. Nixon were in the final stretch of a heated presidential campaign. Both knew King personally. They had talked with him about the issue of equal rights. Two weeks before the election, Kennedy succeeded in getting King released from prison two months early.

When King returned home to Atlanta, he made sure people knew he appreciated Kennedy's help. A few weeks later, Kennedy was elected president of the United States. The Kings' third child, Dexter, was born on January 30, 1961. Their youngest, Bernice, followed on March 28, 1963.

Fair Treatment for Workers

King's fight for equal rights included fair treatment for workers. Blacks were often paid less and worked more hours than their white counterparts. In the 1960s, many labor unions formed to ensure employers treated black workers—and all unfairly treated workers—the same as white workers.

Labor unions had supported King since the days of the Montgomery bus boycott, helping transport the boycotters. On December 11, 1961, King spoke to the American Federation of Labor-Congress of Industrial Organizations, an umbrella organization of various unions more commonly referred to by its initials: AFL-CIO. He tailored his message for the audience, stressing the shared challenges of African Americans and labor unions:

Negroes are almost entirely a working people. Our needs are identical with labor's needs: decent wages, fair working conditions, livable housing, old-age security, and health and welfare measures, conditions in which families can grow, have education for their children, and fight laws that curb labor.[4]

The nonviolent movement was gaining momentum. King was at the forefront of the movement, and other activists began taking up the cause. In 1962, King

FREEDOM RIDERS

In 1961, 13 blacks and whites left Washington, DC, by bus to test how well bus companies in the South were following integration laws. Their plan was to ride to New Orleans, Louisiana. The route would pass through several cities. The passengers, known as Freedom Riders, had little trouble until they reached Alabama. The group faced a mob in Birmingham that burned their bus and attacked some of the riders. Escaping by plane to New Orleans, the group gave up.

Some students in Nashville, Tennessee, had been following the Freedom Riders' progress. They were upset when the protesters gave up the ride. A new group of Freedom Riders left Nashville to complete the journey. An angry mob bent on violence met the second group in Montgomery. King appealed to US Attorney General Robert Kennedy for federal intervention in Alabama for the Freedom Riders. Kennedy sent 400 US marshals to keep the peace in Montgomery. King arrived in the city to counsel the group of young Freedom Riders by leading training meetings. Though King did not play a large role in the Freedom Rides, his intervention protected the group and helped rally public opinion.

appealed to the president for a second emancipation proclamation that would forbid segregation.

The Albany Movement

That year, King also became involved in the Albany Movement, a group based in Albany, Georgia. Members hoped to integrate the public facilities in Albany and gain access for African-American citizens to vote. The organization invited King to speak to gain exposure for its cause.

After an initial protest failed, King brought the full complement of the SCLC to help organize in Albany. Police arrested more than 2,000 African Americans during a variety of marches, petitions, and sit-ins.

In the summer of 1962, the Albany Movement lost energy when it appeared the local government had endless capacity to jail demonstrators. There was no national outrage or sympathy because the local government arrested the demonstrators without violence. The campaign did not end with desegregation, but it helped the SCLC plan future demonstrations.

In late 1962, the civil rights movement was floundering. To help breathe life back into the movement, King met with President Kennedy in early

King spoke with passion at a church in Albany, Georgia, on July 22, 1962.

October to discuss the activist's letter requesting a rededication of the Emancipation Proclamation. The timing could not have been worse. A few days later, world attention turned to a crisis in Cuba, where the Soviet Union had established a base with missiles that could wipe out much of the United States. Kennedy ended the crisis by negotiating with Soviet leader Nikita Khrushchev.

The peaceful resolution of the Cuban Missile Crisis was a great day for the world, but it had turned Kennedy's attention away from civil rights. Events in Alabama in 1963 would turn the world's focus back to the movement.

CHAPTER
SIX

1963: THE YEAR OF BIRMINGHAM

In the early 1960s, living in Birmingham, Alabama, was dangerous. Unknown terrorists bombed so many churches, businesses, and houses that the city was nicknamed "Bombingham."[1]

In 1963, King and his colleagues went to Birmingham. They launched a series of demonstrations with thousands of participants to demand city administrators integrate the city. The idea was to have simultaneous sit-ins, marches, and prayer vigils.

"Letter from Birmingham Jail"

On April 12, 1963, the Friday before Easter, King led a march to downtown Birmingham. The demonstrators linked arms and sang hymns as they walked. The police force had orders to arrest the group. Police placed King in a solitary jail cell, separated from everyone else.

Members of the National States Rights Party opposed to King and the protests in Birmingham sit near an effigy of King they hung outside the party's headquarters in the city.

> "In no sense do I advocate evading or defying the law, as would the rabid segregationist. That would lead to anarchy. One who breaks an unjust law must do so openly, lovingly, and with a willingness to accept the penalty. I submit that an individual who breaks a law that conscience tells him is unjust, and who willingly accepts the penalty of imprisonment in order to arouse the conscience of the community over its injustice, is in reality expressing the highest respect for law."[2]
> —Martin Luther King Jr., "Letter from Birmingham Jail"

Coretta, home in Atlanta with the couple's children, frantically tried to get news of where police had taken her husband. Finally, she called President Kennedy. He convinced local authorities to allow King to see his lawyers and call his wife.

While in custody, King wrote one of his most famous works. A group of eight white clergymen had taken out a newspaper advertisement calling King a troublemaker.

In a letter, King reprimanded the clergymen who wrote the advertisement. He underscored his philosophy of nonviolence and continued passion for civil rights:

> We who engage in nonviolent direct action are not the creators of tension. We merely bring to the surface the hidden tension that is already alive. We bring it out in the open, where it can be seen and dealt with. . . . injustice must be exposed . . . to the light of human

conscience and the air of national opinion before it can be cured.[3]

Many people consider King's "Letter from Birmingham Jail" a manifesto for the civil rights movement and a call to action for blacks and whites alike. Authorities released King after several days.

The Children's Crusade

In 1963, the SCLC was afraid the momentum for the civil rights movement was fading. A local member, James Bevel, came up with the idea to recruit students. He shared his idea with King and the other leaders in the movement. Bevel argued that adults might be afraid of losing their jobs if they participated in demonstrations and that children had less to lose.

The involvement of children in the Birmingham demonstrations made it different from other protests. While King was concerned about sending children into a potentially dangerous situation, he approved of the action.

On May 2, 1963, to protest segregation, thousands of African-American children skipped school and inundated the downtown area of Birmingham. Police arrested more than 1,000 of them. The next day,

> "I like to believe that the negative extremes of Birmingham's past will resolve into the positive and utopian extreme of her future; that the sins of a dark yesterday will be redeemed in the achievements of a bright tomorrow."[4]
> —Martin Luther King Jr.

more children participated in the protest, leaving the city's segregated black schools almost empty. Bull Connor, the city's safety commissioner, ordered the police department to use high-powered water hoses and dogs to control the crowd. A mob of angry adult onlookers ignored King's appeal for nonviolence and threw sticks and stones at the police, escalating the scene into a near riot.

The rioters were not members of King's movement. Still, the event tested his philosophy. His only consolation was that the riot could have been much worse had nonviolence not been his strategy's central theme.

The children's crusade in Birmingham was a turning point for public opinion. News reports and photographs of children attacked by dogs and police officers using high-powered hoses circulated through international news outlets. People around the world were outraged.

The Tide Turns

The demonstrations in Birmingham continued into May. By May 10, the city's business owners began negotiations to desegregate restrooms, lunch counters, and drinking fountains. Meanwhile, angry white racists continued to resist integration of any kind.

Extreme violence continued in Birmingham with more bombings, including the home of King's brother

BOMBING OF THE SIXTEENTH STREET BAPTIST CHURCH

On September 15, 1963, a bomb exploded in the basement of the Sixteenth Street Baptist Church in Birmingham. The church was busy with congregants there for morning worship, preparing for its annual Youth Day celebration.

While adults attended Sunday services in the main part of the church, approximately 80 teenagers met in the basement for Sunday school. The group included Denise McNair, 12; Addie Mae Collins, 14; Cynthia Wesley, 14; and Carol Robertson, 14. The explosion killed the four girls and injured dozens more. It was one of the deadliest acts during the civil rights movement.

The bombing again brought national attention to the civil rights movement—rallying support from blacks and whites alike. The action did not delay integration, as was the intention of the perpetrators.

In 1977, Alabama's state attorney finished a seven-year probe that led to Robert "Dynamite Bob" Chambliss's conviction for murder and possessing dynamite without a permit. Several years later, two coconspirators were charged and convicted. All three men were known members of the KKK. In 2002, a jury of nine blacks and three whites convicted Bobby Frank Cherry, the last living man responsible for the bombing.

and a hotel where King often stayed. These events sparked another riot. Police beat and arrested innocent people. King had gone back to Atlanta to see his family but rushed back to Birmingham to counsel the community not to abandon their nonviolent methods.

The new violence prompted federal intervention. President Kennedy ordered 3,000 federal troops to Birmingham. There was no spontaneous desegregation of Birmingham, but slowly, the situation started improving. Support came from around the world as leaders, entertainers, and athletes spoke out in support of civil rights and equality. Well-known celebrities at its forefront included actors Harry Belafonte, Ossie Davis, and Ruby Dee; athlete Jackie Robinson; and writers Maya Angelou and James Baldwin. Supporters sent money and traveled to the area. King said,

> It was a pride in progress and a conviction that we were going to win. It was a mounting optimism which gave us the feeling that the implacable barriers that confronted us were doomed and already beginning to crumble.[5]

The movement kept moving and with greater force. And King spurred it on.

As King continued being a leader and teacher, as well as a thorn in the side of some Americans, he was always a husband and father.

CHAPTER
SEVEN

THE MOVEMENT GOES NATIONAL

By the summer of 1963, the civil rights movement had gained national attention. This was due in part to the events in Birmingham. In addition, on June 11, President Kennedy unveiled a new bill for Congress's approval guaranteeing civil rights protections for all Americans. He noted, "We are confronted primarily with a moral issue. It is as old as the Scriptures and is as clear as the American Constitution."[1] The forced desegregation of the University of Alabama, which required intervention by the Alabama National Guard, prompted Kennedy's action.

While desegregation gave Kennedy the final push needed to put forth his civil rights bill, civil rights was about more than simply ending segregation. It was about equality. The year 1963 marked the centennial of the Emancipation Proclamation, and African Americans still did not enjoy equality in the United States.

Fred Shuttlesworth, *left*, and Ralph Abernathy, *right*, joined King in leading civil rights activists in Alabama and beyond.

MEDGAR EVERS

On June 12, 1963, the day after Kennedy unveiled his civil rights bill to Congress, civil rights activist Medgar Evers was killed when a bullet struck him outside his home in Jackson, Mississippi. Evers had been a field worker for the NAACP, traveling around Mississippi to help poor African Americans register to vote. A former member of the SCLC, Evers was a proponent of King's strategy of peaceful demonstration.

Evers was buried in Arlington National Cemetery. King and Kennedy attended his funeral. Evers's murder created national outrage and increased support for President Kennedy's proposed bill. After three trials, in 1994, a jury convicted Byron De La Beckwith, a KKK member, of killing Evers.

The unemployment rate among the black community was high, and many who had jobs earned low wages. King and the nation's African-American community were excited about Kennedy's expression of support for the civil rights movement. They hoped it would finally end discrimination and ensure equal opportunities for jobs.

The March on Washington for Jobs and Freedom

To continue the push for social change, King and his colleagues planned a march in Washington, DC. Their goals for the march were to promote a civil rights bill that would end public segregation, protect the right to vote, and create a federal works program to train unemployed workers. They hoped 100,000 people would attend.

Thousands of protesters at the March on Washington for Jobs and Freedom crowded the mall in support of King's fight for equality.

Kennedy did not initially support the march to the Lincoln Memorial. However, King persisted and persuaded the president to give his blessing. In the end, Kennedy hoped it would convince the members of Congress his bill had merit.

On August 28, 1963, the March on Washington for Jobs and Freedom brought together considerably more people than organizers had hoped. A massive crowd of 250,000 people gathered. Blacks, whites, Hispanics, and Asian Americans united to support the cause. The crowd stretched the length of the National Mall to the Washington Monument. Millions more Americans watched the event on television. Attendees at the historic event at the nation's capital included people from different socioeconomic backgrounds and religious faiths. King was thrilled to have more mainstream white clergy participate. He noted, "Never before had [white churches] been so fully, so enthusiastically, so directly involved."[2] In addition to church support, there was a constituency from several labor unions present.

Many performers and speakers took part in the event. Their diversity reflected that of the crowd. Singers included Marian Anderson, Joan Baez, Bob Dylan, and Odetta. Speakers included Joachim Prinz, a rabbi and leader of the American Jewish Congress, and Walter Reuther, president of the Union of Auto Workers.

King was a speaker as well. When it was his turn at the microphone, King started to read lines he had written the night before. He was overwhelmed with emotion. The response from the crowd inspired him to put down his notes and speak from his heart.

Unscripted, he delivered his most famous speech, known today as his "I Have a Dream" speech.

The civil rights leader began by mentioning the Emancipation Proclamation, Lincoln's famous law that ended slavery on January 1, 1863. King continued by noting how, a century later, blacks were far from free because of segregation.

King spoke honestly and passionately. He urged the United States to acknowledge what was happening in

THE EMANCIPATION PROCLAMATION

The election of Abraham Lincoln as president of the United States in November 1860 scared many white southerners. They believed he would end slavery, which was the basis of their way of life. In the months immediately following the election, Alabama, Florida, Georgia, Louisiana, Mississippi, South Carolina, and Texas seceded from the Union. The move led to the Civil War, with the seceding states forming the Confederacy. After the war began on April 12, 1861, Arkansas, North Carolina, Tennessee, and Virginia joined the Confederacy.

In September 1862, Lincoln gave the confederate states an ultimatum. He would grant freedom to every slave in those states unless the states returned to the Union. None took the offer. On January 1, 1863, Lincoln followed through with his threat to the Confederacy. He signed the Emancipation Proclamation, which freed slaves.

Lincoln's proclamation also allowed black soldiers to fight in the Union army, and the army really needed men to help fight. Until the proclamation, Lincoln's goal was to reunite the states—the Emancipation Proclamation also made the war about slavery.

King gives his impassioned and best known speech: "I Have a Dream."

American society and the movement for equality. Then, he spoke the words that gave his speech its name:

> I have a dream that one day this nation will rise up and live out the true meaning of its creed: "We hold these truths to be self-evident: that all men are created equal."[3]

King kept on, expressing what equality looked like in his dream. He concluded his 17-minute heartfelt speech by saying,

> When we let freedom ring . . . we will be able to speed up that day when all of God's children . . . will be able to join hands and sing in the words of the old Negro

spiritual, "Free at last! Free at last! Thank God Almighty, we are free at last!"[4]

Kennedy Assassinated

That fall, the nation seemed on its way toward equality for all Americans. But opponents continued protesting loudly through violence. On November 22, 1963, Lee Harvey Oswald killed Kennedy as the president rode in a motorcade through Dallas, Texas.

King was horrified and sad, but he was not surprised. King had respected Kennedy as a friend and as a leader "unafraid of change."[5] After the assassination, King came to a realization. He said to Coretta, "This is what is going to happen to me also."[6]

Kennedy's assassination did not keep Congress from pushing through his equal

MAN OF THE YEAR

In 1957, *Time* magazine ran a cover story on King and his role in the Montgomery bus boycott. The story called him "the scholarly Negro Baptist minister who in little more than a year has risen from nowhere to become one of the nation's remarkable leaders of men."[7]

Six years later, *Time* named 35-year-old King its "Man of the Year" for 1963. Citing the 250,000 miles (402,336 km) he traveled and 350 speeches he gave, in addition to the struggles in Birmingham and his inspiration to millions, *Time* claimed he was a "symbol of the revolution."[8]

rights bill. On July 2, 1964, the White House invited King to Washington, DC, to attend President Johnson's signing of the bill into law. The Civil Rights Act of 1964 outlawed discrimination in public places and guaranteed school integration. The pen Johnson used to sign the bill into law became one of King's most prized possessions.

Prize for Peace

As King continued fighting for justice and equality for all, many people and groups worldwide recognized the activist for his contributions to civil rights. On December 10, 1964, the Nobel Committee in Norway awarded King the Nobel Prize for Peace. At 35, he was the youngest person to receive the award.

King believed the award was a "testimony to the magnificent drama of the civil rights movement and the thousands of actors who had played their roles extremely well." He added, "It is these 'noble' people who have won this Nobel Prize."[9] As such, he donated the $54,123 in prize money to further fund the civil rights movement. And he continued to push forward, with greater force and support, for change.

King and Coretta hug during a news conference after an announcement that the civil rights leader had been awarded the Nobel Peace Prize.

CHAPTER
EIGHT

SELMA

The acknowledgements King received for his work did not signal the end of his fight for equal and fair treatment for all Americans—far from it. The United States was slowly integrating its public places, but civil rights was much more than desegregating. It was about equality in all arenas, including voting.

In some areas of the country, African Americans still could not vote. In 1964, only 350 of the 15,000 eligible black residents of Dallas County, Alabama, were registered to vote. Without registering, one could not vote. Registering to vote was not always easy, especially in the South. Obstacles included excessive paperwork, long lines, and tests designed to discriminate against African Americans.

King met with President Johnson and members of his administration, hoping to convince them to enact stronger laws protecting people's access to the vote. Johnson agreed. In his State of the Union address on January 4, 1965, the president said, "I propose we

King points to Selma, Alabama, on a map hanging in the office of the SCLC while discussing the organization's plan for protests in the city.

eliminate every remaining obstacle in the right and opportunity to vote."[1]

Focusing on Selma

King and his team wanted to "dramatize the existence of injustice" with regard to voting and to speed up the process to improve it for all eligible Americans.[2] On January 2, 1965, King joined forces with multiple groups to set forth a plan of action, including the SCLC, the Student Nonviolent Coordinating Committee (SNCC), and the Dallas County Voters League. Together with local African Americans, these activists planned a campaign against voting rights inequalities. Specifically, King and his colleagues wanted to attract national attention to the issue of voting rights for African Americans in Selma.

Almost none of Selma's African-American residents—only 2 percent—were registered to vote. Local African Americans already had been pushing for campaign rights along with the SCLC and the SNCC.

Another factor influenced the decision of King and his colleagues to select Selma. The SCLC had been doing work there because local law enforcement had a reputation for violence. If Sheriff Jim Clark and his

In January 1965, African Americans stood in line at the Dallas County Courthouse in Alabama to register to vote.

officers behaved as usual, their brutality would attract the attention of Americans nationwide and bring much-needed focus on the issue of voting rights.

Initially, the activists' work resulted only in arrests, but that changed after a month. In February, police began attacking demonstrators, even though they were passive. On February 18, a state trooper shot a protester. The young man, Jimmie Lee Jackson, died eight days later.

"Bloody Sunday"

A group of 500 demonstrators marched in support of voting rights and in response to the death of their friend and colleague. They set out from Selma on March 7 to walk the 54 miles (87 km) to Montgomery. King was in Atlanta tending to church responsibilities and did not participate, but he spoke to them, stressing the importance of their march:

> I can't promise you won't get beaten; I can't promise you won't get your house bombed; I can't promise that you won't get scarred up a bit, but we must stand up for what is right.[3]

King and his colleagues believed Governor George Wallace would order the protesters arrested. They were wrong. Hosea Williams and John Lewis led marchers. Williams was a member of the SCLC, while Lewis was a leader of the SNCC.

The group walked through Selma and across the Edmund Pettus Bridge. There, they met state troopers who blocked the way. Instead of arresting the protesters, the police attacked them with tear gas grenades and knocked them to the ground. The police clubbed some people. Some mounted officers whipped marchers from their charging horses. White onlookers egged on the attack. Police injured more than 60 protesters, including Lewis, giving the day the name "Bloody Sunday."[4]

News media televised the event, interrupting programming with images of the violence. Millions of Americans saw members of law enforcement attack men and women alike who were trying to march peacefully. Many Americans responded to what they saw with anger. The images would imprint Selma in their minds and bring the issue of voting rights to the national stage.

JOHN LEWIS

John Lewis was born on February 21, 1940, in Troy, Alabama. He has been a dedicated activist for civil rights and fair treatment for all Americans since the early 1960s. As a college student at Fisk University, he organized sit-ins at segregated lunch counters in Nashville, Tennessee. He was also an active participant in the Freedom Rides and risked his life many times by sitting in seats designated for white customers.

As an activist, Lewis was arrested more than 40 times. He was also beaten. As King did, he maintained his devotion to nonviolent demonstration. Lewis helped organize the March on Washington for Jobs and Freedom.

Lewis became a politician. Since 1987, he has served in the US Congress as a representative for Georgia. Lewis has received numerous honors through the years for "his dedication to the highest ethical standards and moral principles."[5] Perhaps his greatest honor was being on the Washington Mall to hear Barack Obama, the first African-American president, give his historic inaugural speeches. Lewis was the only leader from that historic march 45 years earlier still alive and present onstage during the momentous occasion.

A Second March

King was embarrassed he had not been at the march and planned another march for two days later. He reached out to religious leaders nationwide to join him. President Johnson asked King to call off the march until a federal court order could be made to protect participants. King met with his fellow civil rights leaders and a member of the US Justice Department's Civil Rights Division. He decided not to wait for the order, and he proceeded with a second march from Selma to Montgomery.

On March 9, more than 2,000 people gathered, including Catholic nuns and more than 450 clergy members. They were ready to make their way to Montgomery. The protesters met resistance again. Troopers again stopped the marchers at the bridge. To avoid more injuries, King had the group turn back before there was any violence.

A Third March

Two weeks later, with approval from federal judge Frank M. Johnson Jr., civil rights activists tried a third march. The judge approved the plan the protesters submitted detailing the march. His approval prohibited the governor and area law enforcement from attacking protesters in any way.

On March 21, 5,000 people marched out of Selma under protection from the Alabama National Guard and agents from the Federal Bureau of Investigation (FBI). The judge required most of the marchers to stop at the bridge. He allowed 300 protesters to continue along the two-lane highway to Montgomery. The group covered seven to 17 miles (11 to 27 km) each day, camping in supporters' yards along the way.

On March 25, King led the group, which had swelled to thousands, into Montgomery. A few days later, 50,000 people gathered to hear King and others speak. Black, white, Hispanic, and Asian-American activists, from working people to celebrities, joined in support of the movement. King said at the rally,

> There never was a moment in American history more honorable and more inspiring than the pilgrimage of

KING'S WRITINGS

King was a gifted speaker. He was also a talented writer. King wrote several books during his fight for civil rights, including *Stride Toward Freedom: The Montgomery Story* (1958), *Why We Can't Wait* (1963), *Strength to Love* (1963), *Where Do We Go From Here: Chaos or Community?* (1967), *The Trumpet of Conscience* (1968), and *The Autobiography of Martin Luther King Jr.* (1998). Clayborne Carson compiled the autobiography after King's death.

clergymen and laymen of every race and faith pouring into Selma to face danger at the side of its embattled Negroes.[6]

The marchers' efforts were not in vain. In 1965, President Johnson signed the Voter Rights Act, guaranteeing all Americans would have an equal right to vote. But just as the Supreme Court's ruling in *Brown v. Board of Education* in 1954 did not end discrimination, neither did this new law. More work was needed by civil rights activists. King recognized the need to keep moving forward and would expand the movement to other parts of the country.

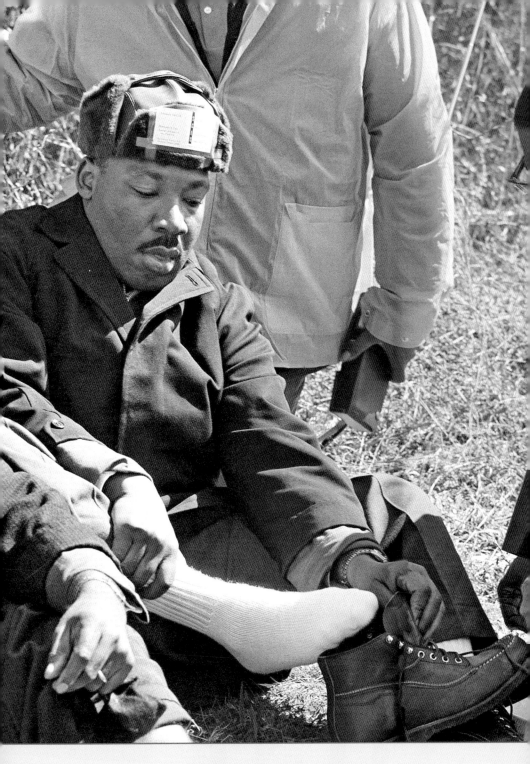

King takes a break on day two of the long
walk from Selma to Montgomery.

CHAPTER
NINE

A GREAT LOSS

In late 1965, King suggested to his SCLC colleagues they expand their focus to other parts of the country. Rioting over unfair treatment had started to break out in major cities, such as Chicago, Illinois.

For several months in 1966, while planning activities for Chicago, King and Coretta lived in a slum apartment there to experience conditions the poor had to endure. King reached out to gang members. Many of them had believed violence was their only option. Some gang members came to embrace the nonviolent movement King revered so much.

"Beyond Vietnam"

After 1966, King turned his attention to issues of poverty, unemployment, and lack of economic opportunity for African Americans. He also spoke out against the Vietnam War.

On April 4, 1967, King gave a speech devoted to his position against the war. In "Beyond Vietnam," he spoke

King and Coretta, *top center*, look out from the window of their apartment in a Chicago slum.

of the destruction the United States caused in Vietnam to families, farms, and Buddhists. He presented five steps the US government could take to end the war, including stopping all bombing and declaring a cease-fire.

Many people did not receive the speech well, including President Johnson, who no longer allowed King to visit the White House. The day after the speech, 168 newspapers wrote stories against King. This speech was more problematic for King than any others he had given.

A New Campaign

King was no stranger to disapproval and did not let it stop him from doing the work he found so important. King began focusing on poverty and economic equality. He wanted a "radical redistribution of economic and political power" and believed the fight would be more challenging than others he and other activists had worked on.[1]

In late 1967, King unveiled one of his most ambitious projects. The plan was to mobilize an army of poor people to march on Washington, DC, and demand the US Congress come up with a plan to end poverty.

King's activism included marching against the Vietnam War, which he did in Chicago in March 1967.

The protesters would not represent a single race. They would be African Americans, Native Americans, Asian Americans, Hispanics, and whites, all fighting together for good. King hoped for 2,000 people to converge on the nation's capitol and demand a fair minimum wage and access to jobs and education.

Despite all that had been accomplished, King knew much more was needed. He moved forward with his vision for the campaign, not knowing he would not live to see his vision come to life.

Going to Memphis

In March 1968, while planning his Poor People's Campaign, King traveled to Memphis, Tennessee,

> "If a man doesn't have a job or an income, he has neither life nor liberty, and the possibility for the pursuit of happiness. He merely exists. We're coming to ask America to be true to the huge promissory note that it signed years ago. And we're coming to engage in dramatic, nonviolent action, to call attention to the gulf between promise and fulfillment, to make the invisible visible."[3]
> —Martin Luther King Jr., in a sermon at the National Cathedral, Washington, DC, March 31, 1968

to participate in a citywide boycott to support striking sanitation workers. They were protesting for better wages and safer working conditions for the mostly African-American staff. They also wanted to unionize, which city officials opposed.

The atmosphere in Memphis was tense. King commuted several times between Memphis and his home in Atlanta. On April 3, 1968, he addressed a crowd of 2,000 people in Memphis. After thanking them for attending, King covered a bit of history, from ancient times to the current day. His speech, as always, was heartfelt and inspired by the enthusiasm of the crowd. He said,

> We've got some difficult days ahead. But it really doesn't matter to me now, because I've been to the mountaintop. . . . I would like to live a long life. . . . But I'm not concerned about that now. I just want to do God's will. . . . I've seen the Promised Land. I may not get there with you. But . . . we, as a people, will get to the Promised Land.[2]

It would be King's last speech. The next day, April 4, as he was getting ready for dinner with friends, King walked onto the balcony at his hotel. As he joked with a friend below in the parking lot, a shot came like a firecracker from a rooming house across from the hotel. The bullet struck King and severed his spinal cord. The civil rights leader died several hours later at the hospital. He was 39 years old.

SUPPORTING CESAR CHAVEZ

As King fought for equal rights for African Americans, Cesar Chavez fought for migrant farm workers, the people who move from place to place to help with agricultural tasks, especially harvesting. Chavez was a Mexican American. He grew up in a family of migrant workers and worked as one, too.

Chavez's devotion and leadership helped bring attention to the difficult conditions in which laborers worked. In 1962, he founded the National Farm Workers Association.

Like King, Chavez was a nonviolent activist. In 1968, he fasted as a passive form of protest. It would be the first of many fasts during his life.

On March 5, King sent Chavez a telegram of support:

I am deeply moved by your courage in fasting as your personal sacrifice for justice through nonviolence. . . . My colleagues and I commend you for your bravery, salute you for your indefatigable work against poverty and injustice and pray for your health and your continuing service as one of the outstanding men of America. The plight of your people and ours is so grave that we all desperately need the inspiring example and effective leadership you have given.[4]

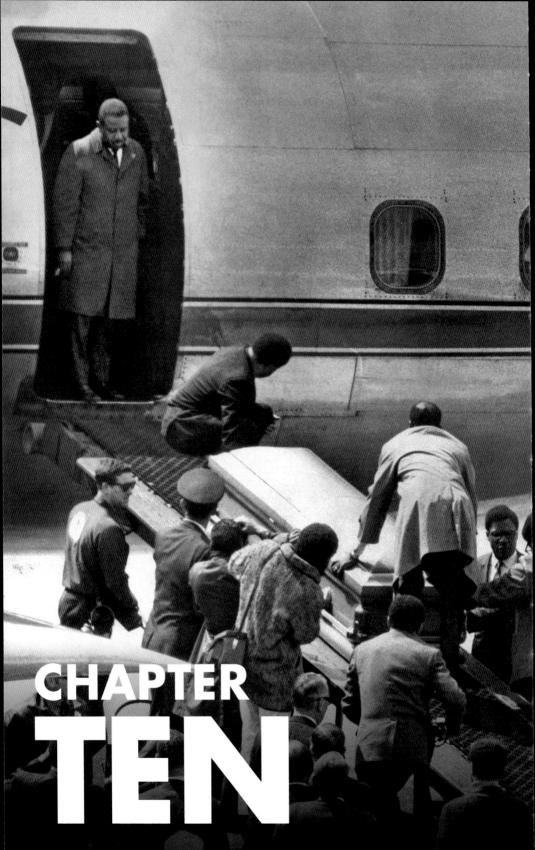

CHAPTER
TEN

AFTERMATH AND LEGACY

King's death rocked the world. In the aftermath of the assassination, riots broke out in major US cities, including Chicago and Washington, DC. People were angry and sad. Regardless of the riots, most people mourned in peace, mindful of King's belief in nonviolence. President Johnson announced April 7 would be a national day of mourning.

Two Funerals

A private funeral service was held for King on April 9 at Ebenezer Baptist Church in Atlanta—the church he attended growing up. Thousands of mourners lined the streets of Atlanta to watch or follow King's casket as it made its way to the church. More than a dozen speakers paid tribute to the fallen activist, including preachers and politicians.

Ralph Abernathy stands in the doorway of a plane, watching the casket of his dear friend being transported onboard to be flown home to Atlanta.

During the service, King gave his own eulogy. A tape recording played of a sermon he had given in February to his congregation at Ebenezer Baptist Church called "Drum Major Instinct." In it, King reflected on this instinct as humans' wish to be first. Humans want to lead the parade just as a drum major does. He discussed the positive and negative results of this tendency. Then, King talked about his death, pondering what he would want people to say at his funeral.

King listed his beliefs and actions. He explained he wanted people to judge him by the values that were most important to him and by which he lived: "I'd like somebody to mention . . . that Martin Luther King Jr. tried to give his life serving others."[1]

Continuing, King applied the idea of the drum major, to himself:

If you want to say that I was a drum major, say that I was a drum major for justice. Say that I was a drum major for peace. I was a drum major for righteousness.[2]

CONSPIRACY THEORY

In 1968, James Earl Ray pled guilty to killing King. He was convicted based on his guilty plea. However, King's family always believed Ray did not act alone. In 1999, a jury in Memphis found that a murder conspiracy headed by an organized crime ring in New Orleans was responsible for King's death, not a lone gunman.

Coretta, *center*, walked in her husband's funeral procession on April 9, 1968, with their children, family, and Ralph Abernathy.

More than 150,000 people came to pay their respects, though the church held only 750. King's remains were placed in a crypt near the church.

Morehouse College, King's alma mater, held a second funeral service, also on April 9. It was for the public. Benjamin Mays, the college president who had become King's mentor, gave a eulogy.

Martin Luther King Holiday

Legislation to make King's birthday a national holiday began almost immediately after his death.

Representative John Conyers Jr. of Michigan introduced the idea to Congress on April 8, 1968.

Three years after King's assassination, the SCLC brought a petition to Congress signed by 3 million people to support the holiday. Steeped in politics, the bill did not go anywhere until President Jimmy Carter supported the idea. In 1979, Coretta spoke before Congress, asking members to support the bill, which missed passing by five votes.

Finally, in 1983, almost 15 years after King's death, President Ronald Reagan signed Martin Luther King Jr. Day into law. Coretta said in response, "This is not a black holiday; it is a people holiday."[3]

Some Americans opposed the law, thinking King should not receive the same recognition as the nation's Founding Fathers by having a holiday in his name. In contrast, many states began recognizing the holiday before it was a federal mandate. However, some states took several years to officially recognize the holiday. The first national celebration occurred on January 20, 1986. That year, 27 states and the District of Columbia honored the holiday. In 2000, South Carolina became the last state to recognize Martin Luther King Jr. Day.

Continuing King's Work

The fight for equal rights and fair treatment did not end with King's death. In 1968, Coretta founded the Martin Luther King Center for Nonviolent Social Change in Atlanta to encourage active learning about King, his accomplishments, and his philosophy of nonviolence.

Coretta continued to be an outspoken proponent of nonviolent protest and worked with the center until her death in 2006. She was a busy social activist, working

THE KING CHILDREN

The King children went on to live productive lives. Some continued their father's work. Yolanda was born on November 17, 1955. She became an actor and motivational speaker. She died at the age of 51 in 2007.

Martin III entered the world on October 23, 1957. Named after his father, he became the president of the SCLC in 1998. He has spread his father's message of nonviolence through workshops in the United States and beyond, visiting countries such as Israel, Kenya, and Sri Lanka. In 2008, Martin and his wife welcomed their first child, the first grandchild of King, Yolanda Renee King.

The Kings' third child, Dexter, was born on January 30, 1961. Following his father, he graduated from Morehouse College. In 2005, Dexter took over leadership of the Martin Luther King Center for Nonviolent Social Change.

The youngest King child, Bernice, was born on March 28, 1963. She earned a law degree and a master of divinity degree. Bernice served as assistant minister of Ebenezer Baptist Church before becoming minister of Greater Rising Star Baptist Church in Atlanta.

for issues such as women's rights and the fight against apartheid in South Africa.

Ralph Abernathy, who had known King since the 1950s and served as King's mentor, took over the leadership of the SCLC when King died. Abernathy died in 1990. Fred Shuttlesworth, King's cofounder of the SCLC, stayed active in ongoing issues related to poverty and race until his death in 2011.

Countless others continued King's work. Their efforts gradually changed opinions and helped continue the social change King started. In 1974, Congress passed the Equal Educational Opportunities Act, which ensures no child is denied access to quality education, regardless of his or her race or national background. Additional positive changes spurred by the civil rights movement include greater opportunities for women, voting rights for Latinos, and immigration reform.

Legacy

Even with all that had been accomplished, as the United States entered a new millennium, it still faced issues of inequality—for people of color, for women, and for homosexuals. The nation took a historic step in 2008 when Americans elected Barack Obama as their first

African-American president. The election of Obama was a celebration of decades of struggle for civil rights activists. An African American finally became president of the United States, the most influential position in the free world. Americans reelected the president in 2012.

Obama was sworn into office a second time on Martin Luther King Jr. Day in January 2013. The year marked the one hundred and fiftieth anniversary of the Emancipation Proclamation and the fiftieth anniversary of the March on Washington for Jobs and Freedom.

Obama honored the legacies of King and Lincoln when he took the oath of president. He placed his hand on a stack of two bibles. They had belonged to Lincoln and King. In his inaugural address, the president stressed the importance of fighting for equality for all marginalized groups. He invoked the memory of King, saying,

All of us are created equal—is the star that guides us still . . . just as it guided all those men and women . . . who left footprints along this great Mall, to hear a preacher say that we cannot walk alone; to hear a King proclaim that our individual freedom is inextricably bound to the freedom of every soul on Earth.[5]

"As we sing the words of belief, 'this is my country,' let us act upon the meaning that everyone is included. May the inherent dignity and inalienable rights of every woman, man, boy, and girl be honored. May all your people, especially the least of these, flourish in our blessed nation. One hundred fifty years after the Emancipation Proclamation and 50 years after the March on Washington, we celebrate the spirit of our ancestors, which has allowed us to move from a nation of unborn hopes and a history of disenfranchised [votes] to today's expression of a more perfect union."[6]
—Myrlie Evers-Williams, widow of slain civil rights leader Medgar Evers, inaugural invocation, January 2013

Almost 45 years since his death, King was still in the thoughts and actions of Americans. His message did not die with him that historic day in 1968 when an assassin cut his life short. Rather, his message lives on, passed between individuals and through laws and institutions.

King fought for all Americans to have equal rights. He inspired others to protest through nonviolent, persistent confrontation. He challenged society and won, but not without sacrifice. He endured discrimination and abuse before paying the ultimate price.

King's words, whether from the pulpit, the street, or his books, galvanized a movement, shaped US history, and changed lives, and they continue to do so today.

His influence continues at many levels, including the highest office in the United States. Martin Luther King Jr. lived and died for his belief in equality and freedom, and his life and work changed—and continue to change—the nation and the world.

TIMELINE

1929
Martin Luther King Jr. is born in Atlanta, Georgia, on January 15.

1948
King is ordained at Ebenezer Baptist Church on February 25.

1953
On June 18, King marries Coretta Scott.

1954
King becomes a full-time pastor of Dexter Avenue Baptist Church on September1.

1955
King receives his PhD from Boston University on June 5.

1955
With King's leadership, the bus boycott begins in Montgomery, Alabama, on December 5.

1956

The Montgomery bus boycott ends successfully on December 21.

1957

The Southern Christian Leadership Conference meets for the first time in January.

1957

At the Prayer Pilgrimage in Washington, DC, on May 17, King addresses a national audience for the first time.

1958

During a book signing in New York City on September 20, Izola Curry stabs King.

1960

King and his family move to Atlanta in February and he becomes assistant pastor of Ebenezer Baptist Church.

1960

In October, police arrest King at a sit-in at Rich's department store and he is jailed for four months.

TIMELINE

1962
King appeals to President John F. Kennedy for a second emancipation proclamation that would forbid segregation.

1963
King is arrested in Birmingham, Alabama, on April 12 and writes his famous "Letter from Birmingham Jail" while in custody.

1963
At the March on Washington for Jobs and Freedom on August 28, King delivers his "I Have a Dream" speech.

1964
King witnesses President Lyndon B. Johnson sign the Civil Rights Act of 1964 into law on July 2.

1964
King receives the Nobel Peace Prize on December 10.

1965

King organizes a march in support of voting rights in Alabama from Selma to Montgomery in March that takes three attempts to complete because of harassment from police.

1967

On April 4, King speaks against the Vietnam War and gains disapproval from many, including President Johnson.

1968

On April 3, King speaks to a crowd in Memphis, Tennessee, in support of sanitation workers in what would become his last speech.

1968

A sniper assassinates King on April 4, shooting him on a hotel balcony in Memphis.

1986

The United States celebrates Martin Luther King Jr. Day as a national holiday for the first time on January 20.

ESSENTIAL FACTS

Date of Birth
January 15, 1929

Place of Birth
Atlanta, Georgia

Date of Death
April 4, 1968

Parents
Alberta King and Martin Luther King Sr.

Education
Morehouse College (bachelor of arts in sociology, 1948),
Crozer Theological Seminary (bachelor of divinity, 1951),
Boston University (PhD, 1955)

Marriage
Coretta Scott (1953)

Children
Yolanda Denise, Martin Luther King III, Dexter Scott,
Bernice Albertine

Career Highlights
King was pastor of the Dexter Avenue Baptist Church in
Montgomery, Alabama, from 1954 to 1958. He also became
president of the Montgomery Improvement Association.

In 1957, he helped form and became president of the Southern Christian Leadership Conference. King served under his father as the assistant pastor of the Ebenezer Baptist Church from 1960 until his death.

King wrote four books and published a collection of his famous sermons. In 1998, a compilation of his writings was released as *The Autobiography of Martin Luther King Jr.*

Societal Contribution

King led the civil rights movement. He promoted nonviolent demonstration to protest inequality. He gave hundreds of speeches, the best known of which is "I Have A Dream." King fought for the rights of others. He lived and died for his belief in equality, and his life and work changed the United States and affected people worldwide.

Conflicts

King's entire career was a series of conflicts. His passive resistance was designed to draw attention to unfair treatment. As a result of his commitment to society's changing mainstream views, he was arrested repeatedly, often because of made-up charges. King's house was bombed on numerous occasions, he was stabbed, and he was threatened often by anonymous letters and phone calls.

Quote

"When we let freedom ring . . . we will be able to speed up that day when all of God's children . . . will be able to join hands and sing in the words of the old Negro spiritual, 'Free at last! Free at last! Thank God Almighty, we are free at last!'"—*Martin Luther King Jr., "I Have a Dream," speech given at the March on Washington, August 28, 1963*

GLOSSARY

alma mater
A school someone has attended or graduated from.

apartheid
A rigid practice of separating people on the basis of race that was practiced in South Africa.

catalyst
Something that causes change.

discrimination
Treating a person differently because of the group to which he or she belongs.

harassment
The repeated bothering or bullying of a person or group.

integration
The bringing together of different groups into a blended group.

legislation
A law.

manifesto
A written statement of an opinion or goals of a person or group.

militant
Vigorously active in support of a cause.

momentous
Historic or memorable.

perpetrator
A person who commits an illegal, criminal, or evil act.

prestigious
Having reputation, influence, or distinction in the eyes of others.

retaliation
Revenge.

revenue
Money earned.

segregation
The separation of one racial group from another or from society.

stereotype
A fixed and oversimplified image or idea of a particular type of person or thing.

unconstitutional
Not allowed according to the US Constitution.

ADDITIONAL RESOURCES

Selected Bibliography

King, Coretta Scott. *My Life with Martin Luther King Jr.* New York: Holt, 1969. Print.

King, Martin Luther, Jr. *The Autobiography of Martin Luther King Jr.* New York: Warner, 1998. Print.

Williams, Donnie and Wayne Greenhaw. *The Thunder of Angels: The Montgomery Bus Boycott and the People Who Broke the Back of Jim Crow.* Chicago, IL: Lawrence Hill, 2006. Print.

Further Readings

King, Martin Luther, Jr. *I Have A Dream.* New York: Schwartz, 2012. Print.

Pastan, Amy. *Martin Luther King Jr.: A Photographic Story of a Life.* New York: DK, 2004. Print.

Pinkney, Andrea. *Hand in Hand: Ten Black Men Who Changed America.* New York: Hyperion, 2012. Print.

Web Sites

To learn more about Martin Luther King Jr., visit ABDO Publishing Company online at **www.abdopublishing.com**. Web sites about Martin Luther King Jr. are featured on our Book Links page. These links are routinely monitored and updated to provide the most current information available.

Places to Visit

Birmingham Civil Rights Institute
520 Sixteenth Street North
Birmingham, AL 35203
205-328-9696, ext. 203
http://www.bcri.org/index.html
The institute houses exhibits and conducts ongoing education
and outreach about the history of the civil rights movement.

**Dexter Avenue King Memorial Baptist Church
(formerly Dexter Avenue Baptist Church)**
454 Dexter Avenue
Montgomery, AL 36104
334-263-3970
http://www.dexterkingmemorial.org
The church where King began his civil rights work is an
important landmark for the Montgomery bus boycott.

The King Center
449 Auburn Avenue NE
Atlanta, GA 30312
404-526-8900
http://www.thekingcenter.org
The King Center houses exhibits and archives of King's
writing and includes the Kings' crypt, King's birth home,
and Ebenezer Baptist Church.

SOURCE NOTES

Chapter 1. The Bus Boycott

1. Coretta Scott King. *My Life with Martin Luther King Jr.* New York: Holt, 1969. Print. 116.

2. Donnie Williams and Wayne Greenhaw. *The Thunder of Angels: The Montgomery Bus Boycott and the People Who Broke the Back of Jim Crow.* Chicago, IL: Lawrence Hill, 2006. Print. 48.

3. Lerone Bennett. *What Manner of Man.* Chicago, IL: Johnson, 1968. Print. 70.

4. "Dr. Martin Luther King, Jr." *NAACP.org.* National Association for the Advancement of Colored People, 2013. Web. 29 Mar. 2012

5. Lerone Bennett. *What Manner of Man.* Chicago, IL: Johnson, 1968. Print. 77.

Chapter 2. Young Martin

1. Martin Luther King Jr. *The Autobiography of Martin Luther King Jr.* New York: Warner, 1998. Print. 5.

2. Lerone Bennett. *What Manner of Man.* Chicago, IL: Johnson, 1968. Print. 20.

3. Martin Luther King Jr. *The Autobiography of Martin Luther King Jr.* New York: Warner, 1998. Print. 10.

4. Lerone Bennett. *What Manner of Man.* Chicago, IL: Johnson, 1968. Print. 27.

5. Ibid.

Chapter 3. Finding a Career, Inspiration, and Love

1. Martin Luther King Jr. *The Autobiography of Martin Luther King Jr.* New York: Warner, 1998. Print. 17.

2. Coretta Scott King. *My Life with Martin Luther King Jr.* New York: Holt, 1969. Print. 97.

Chapter 4. Into the National Spotlight

1. Martin Luther King Jr. *The Autobiography of Martin Luther King Jr.* New York: Warner, 1998. Print. 45.

2. Ibid. 59.

3. Ibid. 54.

4. Martin Luther King Jr. *Birth of a New Age: December 1955–December 1956*. Berkeley, CA: U of California P, 1997. 278. *Google Book Search*. Web. 29 Mar. 2013.

5. Martin Luther King Jr. *The Autobiography of Martin Luther King Jr.* New York: Warner, 1998. Print. 103.

6. Coretta Scott King. *My Life with Martin Luther King Jr.* New York: Holt, 1969. Print. 123.

7. Ibid. 158.

8. Ibid. 162.

Chapter 5. Going to the Next Level

1. Coretta Scott King. *My Life with Martin Luther King Jr.* New York: Holt, 1969. Print. 164.

2. Ibid. 183.

3. Ibid. 188.

4. Martin Luther King Jr. "MLK Address at the AFL-CIO Fourth Constitutional Convention." *TheKingCenter.org*. The King Center, 11 Dec. 1961. Web. 30 Jan. 2013.

Chapter 6. 1963: The Year of Birmingham

1. Mark Gado. "The Birmingham Church Bombing: Bombingham." *Crime Library*. Turner Entertainment, 2013. Web. 28 Mar. 2013.

2. Martin Luther King Jr. "Letter from Birmingham Jail [King, Jr.]." *African Studies Center—University of Pennsylvania*. African Studies Center, 16 Apr. 1963. Web. 28 Mar. 2013.

3. Ibid.

4. "Information." *BCRI.org*. Birmingham Civil Rights Institute, 2013. Web. 28 Mar. 2013.

5. Martin Luther King Jr. *The Autobiography of Martin Luther King Jr.* New York: Warner, 1998. Print. 210.

Chapter 7. The Movement Goes National

1. John F. Kennedy. "Civil Rights Announcement, 1963." *American Experience: Primary Resources*. WGBH Educational Foundation, PBS, 2010. Web. 28 Mar. 2013.

SOURCE NOTES CONTINUED

2. Martin Luther King Jr. *The Autobiography of Martin Luther King Jr.* New York: Warner, 1998. Print. 222.

3. "Dr. Martin Luther King." *NAACP.org.* National Association for the Advancement of Colored People, 2013. Web. 29 Mar. 2012.

4. Martin Luther King Jr. "I Have a Dream, 1963." *American Experience: Primary Resources.* WGBH Educational Foundation, PBS, 2010. Web. 29 Mar. 2013.

5. Martin Luther King Jr. *The Autobiography of Martin Luther King Jr.* New York: Warner, 1998. Print. 237.

6. "King Had Predicted He Too Would Be Killed—like JFK." *Washington Afro-American,* 9 Sept. 1969. *Google News Search.* Web. 23 Nov. 2012.

7. Coretta Scott King. *My Life with Martin Luther King Jr.* New York: Holt, 1969. Print. 152.

8. "America's Gandhi: Rev. Martin Luther King Jr." *Time.com.* Time Inc., 3 Jan. 1964. Web. 28 Mar. 2013.

9. Harry G. Lefever. *Undaunted by the Fight: Spelman College and the Civil Rights Movement, 1957–1967.* Macon, GA: Mercer UP, 2005. 219. *Google Book Search.* Web. 29 Mar. 2013.

Chapter 8. Selma

1. Martin Luther King Jr. *The Autobiography of Martin Luther King Jr.* New York: Warner, 1998. Print. 276.

2. Ibid. 277.

3. Coretta Scott King. *My Life with Martin Luther King Jr.* New York: Holt, 1969. Print. 259.

4. Ibid. 260.

5. "Biography." *Congressman John Lewis: Representing Georgia's 5th District.* N.p., n.d. Web. 29 Mar. 2013.

6. "Selma to Montgomery March (1965)." *Martin Luther King Jr. and the Global Freedom Struggle.* Stanford University: Martin Luther King Jr. Research and Education Institute, n.d. Web. 29 Mar. 2013.

7. Coretta Scott King. *My Life with Martin Luther King Jr.* New York: Holt, 1969. Print. 153.

Chapter 9. A Great Loss

1. "New Front in the Fight for Freedom." *American RadioWorks: King's Last March*. American Public Media, 2013. Web. 29 Mar. 2013.

2. Coretta Scott King. *My Life with Martin Luther King Jr.* New York: Holt, 1969. Print. 316.

3. "Poverty, Martin Luther King's Last Cause." 16 Oct. 2011. *NPR.org*. NPR, 2011. Web. 29 Mar. 2013.

4. Martin Luther King Jr. "Telegram from MLK to Cesar Chavez." *TheKingCenter.org*. The King Center, 3 Mar. 1968. Web. 30 January 2013.

Chapter 10. Aftermath and Legacy

1. "From the Pulpit to the Heart." *American RadioWorks: King's Last March*. American Public Media, 2013. Web. 29 Mar. 2013.

2. Ibid.

3. Frances Romero. "A Brief History of Martin Luther King Jr. Day." 18 Jan. 2010. *Time.com*. Time Inc., 2013. Web. 29 Mar. 2013.

4. Martin Luther King Jr. *The Papers of Martin Luther King, Jr.: Volume IV: Symbol of the Movement, January 1957–December 1958*. Berkeley, CA: U of California P, 1997. 88. *Google Book Search*. Web. 29 Mar. 2013.

5. Barack Obama. "Transcript: President Obama 2013 Inaugural Address." 21 Jan. 2013. *WashingtonPost.com*. Washington Post, 21 Jan. 2013. Web. 29 Mar. 2013.

6. Jamil Smith. "Myrlie Evers-Williams' Invocation a Nod to Civil Rights Struggles Old and New." *tv.msnbc.com*. NBCUniversal, 21 Jan. 2013. Web. 29 Mar. 2013.

INDEX

ABOUT THE AUTHOR

Kristine Carlson Asselin is the author of more than a dozen children's books for the elementary school and library market. In addition to nonfiction, she writes young-adult and middle-grade fiction. She has a BS from Fitchburg State University and an MA from the University of Connecticut. She lives with her husband and daughter in a suburb of Boston.

ABOUT THE CONSULTANT

Paul Ortiz has a PhD in history from Duke University and is associate professor of history at the University of Florida. He is also director of the University of Florida's Samuel Proctor Oral History Program, which strives to capture and encourage living history of people of all kinds. He wrote *Emancipation Betrayed: The Hidden History of Black Organizing and White Violence in Florida from Reconstruction to the Bloody Election of 1920* (2005) and co-edited and conducted interviews for *Remembering Jim Crow: African Americans Tell About Life in the Jim Crow South* (2008). Ortiz is passionate about history and enjoys sharing that passion and his knowledge with students of all ages.